D A I

(ENOUGH)

DAI

(ENOUGH)

A PLAY

Iris Bahr

NORTHWESTERN UNIVERSITY PRESS
EVANSTON, ILLINOIS

Northwestern University Press
www.nupress.northwestern.edu

Copyright © 2006 by Iris Bahr. Pub-
lished 2009 by Northwestern University
Press. All rights reserved.

DAI production photography on pages
75–78 copyright © 2009 by Bruce Glikas.

Printed in the United States of America
10 9 8 7 6 5 4 3 2 1

Library of Congress Cataloging-in-
Publication Data

Bahr, Iris.
    DAI : (enough) / Iris Bahr.
       p. cm.
    "DAI premiered at the Culture
Project in New York City in fall 2006
(Allan Buchman, producer) and ran
through March 2007, starring Iris Bahr
in all roles."
    ISBN 978-0-8101-2643-5 (pbk. :
alk. paper)
    1. Suicide bombers—Israel—
Drama. 2. Arab-Israeli conflict—
Drama. I. Title.
    PS3602.A47D35 2009
    812.6—dc22

                            2009024606

∞The paper used in this publication
meets the minimum requirements of the
American National Standard for Infor-
mation Sciences—Permanence of Paper
for Printed Library Materials, ANSI
Z39.48-1992.

CONTENTS

A NOTE FROM THE PLAYWRIGHT

I have never been one of those people who hunger to discuss the Israeli-Palestinian conflict, if only because I find that most such "discussions" are just shouting matches between people whose minds have already been made up; listening is nonexistent, food is flung, and historical facts are tossed about like ego-filled "I'm right!" confetti.

Even the most enlightened discourse always seems to descend into a flurry of defensiveness and frustration. I've seen it happen countless times, and I usually find myself sucked into the fray, bouncing between both sides of the "discussion," which almost always unfolds in the same fashion: Side *A* begins by expressing compassion for the Palestinian people, mourning the loss of innocent life on both sides, whereupon *B* states human rights abuse and occupation as the cause. "We want a two-state solution, Hamas wants us obliterated!" *A* testily replies, throwing in something about the tragedy of bad leadership that doesn't serve its people, while *B* yells back something about disproportionate military reactions, invoking the whole stones-versus-tanks argument. *A* retorts that the so-called victims are actually the aggressors and reminds *B* of the time Arafat turned a perfectly fair deal down. *B* then turns red with anger and cries, "Fair for who?" protesting settlements and land grabbing. *A* cites the Bible and the history of the land, *B* snaps back with a different history of the land, and so on and so forth until both sides are so emotionally drained they realize they stopped listening three dehumanizing yells ago.

One thing I know for certain: the conflict waxes and wanes, fades in and out of tragedy on both sides, and I am left, like many Israelis, with my heart and head fluctuating between *A* and *B* (and *C, D,* and *E* ...) on a daily basis. *DAI* was born out of my need to express these conflicting opinions and emotions—the desire to explore not only the splintered Israeli psyche but various outsiders' experience of that psyche, to create characters that would bring to life the diverse Israeli society that I have experienced in times of conflict as well as calm, a society that deals not only with Israel-specific issues of religion and national identity, Zionism and post-Zionism and the price of peace, but with universal issues of love, loss, family, and heartbreak.

I hope my stories will entertain, illuminate, humanize, and perhaps lessen the food flinging, just a little bit. Thank you.

Iris Bahr

PRODUCTION HISTORY

DAI premiered at the Culture Project in New York City in fall 2006 and ran through March 2007, starring Iris Bahr in all roles.

Producer . . . . Allan Buchman
Director . . . . Will Pomerantz
Sound design . . . . Frank Gaeta
Lighting and set design . . . . Garin Marshall

In May 2007, Iris Bahr performed *DAI* at the United Nations for over a hundred ambassadors and delegates. In August 2007, she performed *DAI* at the Edinburgh Festival, where she was nominated for the UK Stage Award for Best Solo Performance.

DAI subsequently reopened in New York City at the Forty-Seventh Street Theatre and ran from November 2007 through March 2008, starring Iris Bahr in all roles.

Producers . . . . Bernie Kukoff, Jon Pollard,
            Jon Cutler, and Highbrow Entertainment
Sound design . . . . Frank Gaeta
Lighting and set design . . . . Marc Janowitz

DAI was nominated for two Drama Desk Awards, for Outstanding Solo Performance and Outstanding Sound Design, in 2007, and two Lucille Lortel Awards, for Outstanding Solo Show and Outstanding Sound Design, in 2008.

In 2008, it won the Lortel Award for Outstanding Solo Show.

Bahr has since been touring with her show around the world, including sold-out runs in London, Tel Aviv, Los Angeles, Washington, D.C., and San Francisco.

DAI

(ENOUGH)

CHARACTERS

Christiane Saloniki, *British TV reporter of Middle Eastern descent*

Jessica Mendoza, *American Latina actress*

Uzi Karabelnik, *Israeli kibbutznik*

Alma Yalin, *Israeli expat New Yorker*

Shuli Feinstein, *Brooklyn-born West Bank settler*

Hendrik Niggeman, *German furniture designer*

Svetlana, *Russian prostitute*

Trev Brodman, *American Christian evangelist*

Rebecca, *American volunteer in the Israeli army*

Avivit, *Israeli raver chick*

Nijma Aziz, *Palestinian professor*

(This is a solo show. Although other characters may be addressed or otherwise indicated in the stage directions, only one actor is present on the stage throughout the play.)

PERFORMANCE NOTE

The actor's body during the transitions should be neutral, that is, once a character's costume is removed during the death sequence, the actor goes into a neutral state that is sustained until the next character's costume is reached, at which point the transformation into that next character begins.

LIGHTS

The café general wash should be warm and welcoming. At the moment of each explosion, the entire café should go dark save for a lone spotlight on the current character, who dies in that instant. These "death lights" vary in shape and size depending on the angle at which they hit the victim, at times resembling white coffins of sorts.

The lights during the transitions between characters should be neutral yet dramatic, preferably shins that create strong shadows and highlight the moving silhouette.

SOUND

The sound effect of the bombing and its immediate aftermath should be as realistic as possible and should incorporate additional elements each time. The volume should be loud enough to seriously jolt the audience out of their seats and must per-meate the entire space, enveloping the audience from all sides.

I have found that the numerous repetitions of the bombing af-fect each member of the audience differently: some become increasingly sensitized and anxious with each bombing and subsequent death, while others grow more desensitized; some find themselves annoyed at being shaken up so harshly; others find the tension of not knowing when the next explosion will occur intolerable. All are welcome reactions to the horrible na-ture of the event and in a way mirror what happens to people living in societies plagued by bombings on civilians.

SET

The café set should be minimal, comprising solely three round black café tables downstage and two café tables upstage. Two bent wood café chairs stand at each table (except for Alma's table, which has only one chair). Two baby strollers rest mid-stage right.

The costumes are draped over the various chairs, like empty human shells. Shuli's costume is draped over the baby strollers.

Downstage left table: Uzi and Nijma
On the table are a coffee mug, a Jimi Hendrix CD,
a handwritten note, and a cell phone.

Downstage center table: Hendrik
On the table are an espresso cup, a pair of glasses, and a
cabbie hat.

Downstage right table: Alma
On the table are cigarettes, an ashtray, a cell phone, and a
pair of sunglasses.

Upstage left table: Svetlana, Trev
On the table are blueprints, a cell phone, a blonde wig, and
trance flyers.

Upstage right table: Rebecca, Jessica
On the table are four mugs on a tray, a script, and a Bluetooth.

[*Lights up on a bustling café in Tel Aviv, present day.* CHRISTIANE SALONIKI, *an androgynous, icy, well-groomed British TV reporter in her forties, stands outside the café with her crew. She whispers into her cell phone, frustrated.*]

CHRISTIANE SALONIKI: No— No—Peter, we've been through this a million times. Nobody *cares* what the Israelis have to say, they live like kings. Can you hear the café? It's like a bloody party!

No, people want to know how the *victims* are feeling. Well, the Israelis can't really be defined as that, can they . . . How could I be anti-Semitic, Peter—I'm part Syrian. Well, then don't use terms like "anti-Semitic"; that's not just Jews, that's all Semitic populations . . . No, the weather is actually quite lov— Is that what that Jewish bitch Sharon told you—that I'm anti-Semitic?! One piece of mine on Lebanon and I'm *still* paying for it . . . Well, I didn't call *her* a Nazi, now, did I? . . .

No, it is an apt comparison if severe human rights abuse and mass *murder* is your paramet—I don't care if they're outraged —No . . . No—Yes, yes, fine, I understand, "my job is in question." I will *talk* to the people here, we will *get it* on camera, you will *have* your bloody piece, whereupon you will meet me in London impregnate me and marry me in that order.

[*A beat.*]

Well, why the hell not, Peter.

[CHRISTIANE *takes a step away from the crew and mouths "Sorry."*]

Can we not talk about this now? I know *I* did, but *I* don't think I can handle the answer. No, I can't express my needs in a calm fashion, you fucking asshole, I LOVE YOU!

[CHRISTIANE *hangs up.*]

Bloody prick.

[*To the crew, as she positions herself in front of the café*] All right, let's do this. Am I all right over here—we get the whole café? [*Groaning under her breath*] God.

[CHRISTIANE *turns unenthused to her cameraman and motions for him to start rolling. She looks into camera and launches into her deep-voiced, earnest "reporter mode."*]

Hello, Diane. Right now I'm at a bustling café in Tel Aviv as part of my mission to explore the Israeli plight, which has been largely unexamined and unjustifiably so. I'll be talking to the man and woman of the Israeli street, to provide an in-depth look into the mind of the average Israeli, who lives and breathes existential threat—a threat that has increased exponentially since Hamas came into power, Iran became a force to be reckoned with, and, for the first time, Israel proved to be no match for its enemies.

Let me add, Diane, that I am aware of the "criticism" I have come under as of late, and I *am* committed to showing both sides of every story, which is why after six months in Beirut and Gaza, I'm here to see how the *other* side feels.

[*To cameraman*] Cut!

[CHRISTIANE's *face goes sour. She enters the café and scans the patrons, the crew trailing behind her.*]

Well, aren't they lovely. All right, let's find some people that are sitting alone; they're more apt to talk to us.

[CHRISTIANE *spots a young woman in the corner.*]

Ooh, that one, in the blue sweatshirt. Peter loves those cheesy types. Must be an "actress."

[*Light change, a Jimi Hendrix–style riff sounds through the café as*

CHRISTIANE *approaches the upstage right table where her first inter-viewee's clothes await.* CHRISTIANE *removes her safari jacket in a frigid fashion and morphs into* JESSICA MENDOZA, *twenty-two, a pretty, young American actress in a baby-blue Juicy Couture velour tracksuit and Kangol hat.*]

[*Café lights up.*]

[JESSICA's *on her Bluetooth, talking a mile a minute to her best friend in Los Angeles. She speaks in a self-righteous tone that screams, "I think I'm a lot smarter and more well read than I am in actuality."*]

JESSICA MENDOZA: First class from LAX—can you *believe* it?! Well, that's what a good production does, Karen, they fly you out to do the research!

Well, no, what was I gonna tell them—"Hi, Mr. Oscar-Winning Director, I'm part Puerto Rican, part Dominican?!" I mean the role's Israeli, I told him I was Israeli! Well, that's what you have to *do*, Karen. Well, yeah, he was like, "What's up with your last name?" And I said, "It's not *really* Mendoza. My father changed it from Mendel to Mendoza when he left Jerusalem for Brooklyn."

Yeah, totally bought it!

[JESSICA *turns to see Christiane hovering in her personal space.*]

Hold on a second, Karen. [*To Christiane*] I'm sorry? [*Back to*

Karen] Oh, how funny, they want to interview me. And the film hasn't even come out yet! [*Giving Christiane the hand*] Yeah, that's fine, just give me a coupla minutes.

[JESSICA *turns away and eagerly gets back to Karen, pacing through the café as if it were her living room.*]

I know, I didn't think I was gonna do it either. I said I'd only do this movie if I agreed with its message, you know? I can't support the double standard America exercises on a daily basis! The way we look down on Arab countries, think we're better than they are . . . subcivilizations that we can imperialize and colonize at will, right? Totally!

I mean, you should see this place, Karen. It's *booming*. And then you drive an hour south of here and there are refugee camps with no running water and it breeds desperation, I know it does!

[*She scans the café.*]

Ugh, I could never live here. The women are gorgeous. Who wants to worry about that kind of shit all the time.

Look, I'm not saying Israel doesn't have the right to exist, I mean, who determines *that* right really, you know? But why put your country *here*? I mean, we as a people, as a nation, we Americans pride ourselves on taking people in and letting them be themselves. So why not just come live in America and cause less problems for your neighbors?! I should tell these people, "Why cram yourself in a tiny space near the Mediterranean surrounded by people that hate you—come to Phoenix!"

Phoenix is funny, right? So's Pittsburgh. My agent always told me if I want to make a joke with a city in it, it should always be Phoenix or Pittsburgh. No, Houston doesn't work, Karen. [*Annoyed*] Okay . . . "Why cram yourself in a tiny space surrounded by people that hate you—come to Houston!" See, it doesn't work!

What? Oh, right, the script!

[JESSICA *skips over to her table, where a script lies open.*]

Well, they were keeping it confidential, Karen; even *I* didn't know what it was about. [*Excited*] This movie is going to be a political beacon for the masses and it's *totally* gonna take my career to the next level!!

Well . . . it's a love story. Between a Palestinian boy—you know, down in the dumps, no job . . . on the verge of being recruited to be a suicide bomber . . . hates Israel—hates Israelis with a passion, yeah, he's turned them into one amorphous enemy and he's on the brink, he's ready to join the ranks of the revered suicide bombers. Oh my God, *totally* revered, are you kidding me?! There's posters of these guys everywhere: on the streets, in classrooms, in kindergartens— they're like Elvis, these guys! And this guy, Youssef, he's ready for his *own* poster, you know what I mean?

And that's all by page twenty! Really. Tight. Writing. By page twenty-four, he's geared up and ready to go. There's a scene of him strapping on the explosives and putting on this really nice suit to kinda *blend* in . . .

And he gets a cab ride out of the Occupied Territories from this Russian cabdriver—the *Occupied Territories*, Karen. The West Bank, Gaza. It might even be East Jerusalem because I was *just* informed that's occupied too!

Anyway, this Russian cabdriver's getting paid a lot of money from the Hamas to be the transpo guy. No, they're not *unionized*, Karen.

Well, of course he knows he's transporting a bomber, but he could care less. He's only in Israel to make money—he has no allegiance to either side. His wife is the breadwinner and he's *over* it! She's a prostitute. She only has a coupla lines, Karen. No, they want a real Russian, okay? I'm sorry. [*In babying voice*] You know I support your acting career, right? Okay.

Well, we cut to Youssef getting to Tel Aviv. Now get this—the café scene is the climax. The D.P. was the camera operator on *The Matrix*, so he's gonna shoot everything really choppy and sweepy at the same time, and the music's gonna have all this really weird exotic singing, kinda like on the *Gladiator* sound track.

[JESSICA *bursts into "ethnic" song—think Lisa Gerard meets* American Idol—*with some awkward Moroccan-style intonations to boot. She loses herself in a mild ethnic frenzy of sorts before realizing some patrons are staring at her, confused.*]

Sorry. Sorry about that.

Anyway, Youssef walks right into the café, he just *breezes* on in, and sitting there is this beautiful Israeli girl—that's me—who's waiting for some Internet date named Shmulike or something, I have to get the pronunciations down. My dialect coach worked on *Munich,* Karen. I'm not worried!

Anyway, he sees me, and suddenly he's aroused—amongst all his nervousness and determination he's suddenly distracted from his mission. You know how guys are when they get boners, even a suicide mission takes a backseat! And *I'm* looking at this guy, thinking, "Wow. He's kinda cute in a scruffy, edgy, East Villagey kind of way . . ." So I smile at him. And that smile? It raises doubt. Yeah, suddenly he's debating, "Do I blow myself up, or do I go join this beautiful Israeli girl for coffee? Not that I would, because I'm *Palestinian* and she's *Israeli,* but what if I *did,* you know? What if I put the bomb switch on pause, walked up to her, and asked her if I could join her for coffee? Would she say yes? What if she said no— Is it because I'm Palestinian, or because she doesn't like me as a man, as a body type? If I were Israeli would she have said no just the same? How will I ever know?!!

You know what, Karen, the lines in the script are a lot more powerful. Stand by.

[JESSICA *leaps back over to the table where the script awaits, she searches through it eagerly.*]

I'm not going to do the accent now, though. Okay.

[JESSICA *finds the page, she goes into her best "man stance" as Youssef, and reads from the script.*]

"What would fucking her be like"—I told you it was *edgy*! "What would fucking a Jewish girl be like— Sweet? Sour? Would the hate overpower the pleasure, or would the pleasure overpower the hate? What would I feel as I entered her, as I came inside her . . . Would she look me in the eye the way she is looking now? She's still looking . . . She's still smiling . . ."

Anyway, he decides to ask her. If he could *join her for coffee,* Karen. You know I'm paying a shitload in roaming charges, the least you can do is listen!

He says to himself, "If she says yes, if her smile is really an invitation, then I'll join her for coffee and *not* blow myself up," right? But if she says no, then *flick* goes the switch and *boom!* the music gets louder and body parts are flying and it's intense, it's really, really intense!

So he puts his finger on the switch and starts walking to-wards me, right? Now at this point, I'm thinking, "Shit, this must be my Internet date!" I mean nobody ever looks like their photos online *anyway,* and he may be overdressed for summer, but he's got this beautiful olive skin and these huge, brown, sensual eyes—I mean I'm psyched, I'm still smiling!

So he walks right up to me, Karen, and he gets really close, I mean we're breathing on each other, Karen, we're *breathing* . . . and he says to me really sweetly, "Can I join you for coffee?" and then I say . . .

[JESSICA *waits a few beats, reveling in the tension she's created.*]

Well, I *can't* tell you what I say, Karen, cuz then you'll know how the movie ends and before I know it, the whole *world* knows how the movie ends and ticket sales go in the kaka bin! And then that Bin Laden biopic with Ben Kingsley comes out and we're fucked. Well, you can't keep a secret, Karen. Oh, really? Remember when you told everyone I had HPV? I can't risk it. Look, let's just say there's a sex scene, but no sequel, okay?

Well, we start shooting in Romania next week. Nobody would shoot the movie here, Karen, it's too dangerous. Why do you think they were so impressed by me that I wanted to actually come here and do some research? I mean, some actors think that losing forty pounds for some Sundance indie flick about dysfunctional family life in Westport, Connecticut, is commitment, but come on! I'm the real artist here. I mean, I put myself in harm's way. This is where the real drama hap—

[*Explosion. A massive blast rips through the space. Screams, chaos, shattered glass.*]

[*All goes horribly dark, save for* JESSICA, *who collapses into a coffin of white light. She lies there lifeless as the cacophony around her con-*

tinues. After a few beats, she slowly sits up and dramatically removes her clothes in an Oscar-worthy fashion.]

[*As the Israeli folk song "Erev Shel Shoshanim" begins to sound through the din,* JESSICA *crawls over to the center stage chair, where she morphs into* UZI KARABELNIK, *a portly kibbutznik with a heavy gait and a body condensed by years of farming and combat.*]

[UZI, *in his sixties, is a tried-and-true, salt-of-the-earth Zionist with a warm demeanor and a loving yet pained gleam in his eye. He shuffles across the café toward another table downstage left and takes a seat. On the table are a Jimi Hendrix CD, a small handwritten note, an outdated cell phone, and a coffee mug.*]

[*Café lights up.*]

[UZI *amusedly watches Christiane roam about with her crew. His voice is deep and booming. He speaks with a heavy Israeli accent, tinged with a slight lisp. A hearty laugh punctuates his speech throughout.*]

UZI KARABELNIK: *Hallo! Tizahari sham im hakabelim, kacha korot teunot!* [Be careful with the electric cords, that's how accidents happen!]

Oh, I'm sorry—you are a journalist . . . [*chuckling*]. My English is not so good.

CNN? CNN? My son will be here in ten minutes, you should interview him, because once he is drafted into the army next week, he is not allowed to talk to press. Yes, he is going to 669, the most *elite unit in the Israeli military*! But until then he is spending all this time with his girlfriend, Dannah, here in Tel Aviv, so I have to come here to see him, but it's okay. I get to see my other son, Gadi, as well.

Ah? We are from Kibbutz Lehavot Habashan, you know?

He-heh, of course not. We are at the end of the world! You know, it's so funny, a few weeks ago, a producer is calling me from Los Angeles—you know Los Angeles, yes? I remember him on the kibbutz as a young boy. We used to call him Panas. Eh . . . flashlight. Because he was so white we could see him coming out of the chicken coop in the middle of the night from a kilometer away!

This producer is saying to me, "Uzi, we are making a movie about the Middle East conflict." I said, "Israel?" He said, "Yes." I said, "Since when are we the entire Middle East? We are a tiny dot! You'd think we were kings of the planet with all the drama!"

He is so excited, he is saying, "Wow . . . soldiers getting kidnapped, a war in Lebanon, I can't believe you haven't made a movie about it yet." I said, "You Americans are so funny, you have one war in Vietnam, you are making five hundred movies about it. A prime minister gets assassinated, you are already thinking which actor will play him before he is even buried in the ground!"

Yes, he was calling to consult with me because they are portraying Arik's unit. Arik Shar—Ariel Sharon, yes. We were in the same unit in '67, '73 . . . I saw him an hour ago, he is in the room next to my son's.

[*Christiane notices the CD.*]

Ah, this? This is, eh, Jimi Hendrickson. Sorry Hendrix, Hendrix! Gadi always made fun of me for getting the name wrong. He loves this music, you can see his eyelids move when he is hearing it, he is getting so excited!

[UZI's *cell phone rings.*]

Sorry, it's my wife, Miri. [*Into the phone*] *Hallo? Ken Mirileh. Heveti lo et ha Hendrixon. Lo, hu lo ohev Banai Miri. Miri al tivki li achshav, ein li koach lezeh. Miri maspik. Maspik. MASPIK!* [Yes, Mirileh. I brought him the Hendrickson. He doesn't like Ehud Banai. Don't start crying, Miri. I don't have the energy for this. Miri, enough. Enough. ENOUGH!]

[UZI *slams the phone shut, then tries to downplay his outburst.*]

Heh, my wife gets emotional from nothing. She sees an advertisement for allergy pills she starts to cry!

[UZI *pauses for a moment; he smiles shyly.*]

I'll call her back. [*Into phone*] *Mirileh, ani miztaer shetzaakti, at yodaat eich ani achrei she ani mevaker oto. Lo, ani eheyeh be-*

miluim. [I'm sorry I yelled at you, you know how I get after I visit him. No, I can't . . . I'll be on reserve duty.]

Okay. [*Making funny kissing sounds*] Poopoopoo. Poopoopoopoopoo. Bye-bye.

[*He puts the phone down, gently this time.*]

My wife says to me, "Uzi, you have lost your emotions, I am tired of looking for them." I tell her, "Miri, you have enough emotions for the two of us, and what good is it doing you? You are thin as a stick, you don't have *energia* to visit Gadi in the hospital, how will you have *energia* to take Amir to the *bakum* next week? The *bakum* . . . the basic training collection place. [*Glowing with pride*] He is going to 669, the most *elite unit in the Israeli military*—same unit as Gadi!

[*Christiane asks about the note.*]

You are a good reporter, ah—many questions, many questions!

[UZI *picks up the paper ever so gently with his large hands, his speech slows.*]

Eh . . . this is a poem that Amir gave to me . . . four hours after the *Ramatkal,* the chief commander—the chief of staff—came to tell us that Gadi had been shot in the head.

[A beat.]

At first, when Miri saw the *Ramatkal's* car drive up to our house, she thought he was just coming by to say hello. After all, he was in the same unit with me and Arik, and every time he was in the Golan he would stop by.

So, Miri ran to the kitchen to make coffee, I put down the volume of the football game on the television. But when I heard him open the gate, I *knew* something was wrong. His army boots—I remember them in the field, they were always light like a feather, almost *gliding* over the dirt. But that day, it sounded like he was four hundred kilo heavy, his boots dragging the ground like a tractor. A distance of ten meters took him five minutes. By the time he called my name from outside the door . . . I knew.

His voice was like paper, the same voice that boomed over the snow and mountains of Lebanon, was now like cracked paper. *"Uzi, tiftach et hadelet!"* [Uzi, open the door!] *"Patuach,"* I said, unable to move from my chair, my finger still on the mute button.

*[*UZI *takes a breath that's deeper than he'd like to admit.]*

Amir did not come out of his room for hours, quiet. The only sound was Mirileh screaming. I was still holding her on the sofa when Amir came out of his room four hours later. He did not say a word, he just gave me this poem. And every time I visit Gadi in the hospital I have to read it to myself.

[UZI *chuckles awkwardly.*]

It's by Rachel. You know her? *Heh,* of course not. She was from Kibbutz Dganiah, the first kibbutz. Came to this country even before my grandparents came, thinking everything will be all right. They *had* to think everything will be all right, after what they went through in Treblinka and Majdanek—the body could not function any other way. After such trauma the brain floods the body with hope, beyond reason or rationality, otherwise it will just die!

    I'm sorry? I do not understand the question. [*Annoyed*] No, please *repeat* the question. [*In disbelief*] You think because one son was injured, that gives my family the right for the other son to not serve?! You are like Miri, living in a fantasy world—no sacrifice, no obligations. Every second family in our kibbutz has lost someone in the army! We owe it to our country to keep protecting, to *keep protecting*! The Arabs put down their weapons, no more war, we put down our weapons, NO MORE ISRAEL! YOU HAVE HEARD OF THIS?!!!

[UZI *looks at his watch.*]

Achh. Amir is late. It is not like him, he knows a time is a time, the army will not tolerate such behavior!

[*The phone rings.* UZI's *face lights up.*]

Ah, he is a responsible boy. [*Into phone*] Hallo? *Ken Amirkeh, eifo atah? Az lama ata lo nichnas?* [*Shocked*] *Lehagid li ma? Mi zot Dana machnisa lechah et hashtuyot haeleh? Ma New York!? Ata mitgayes shavua haba, ata oseh tzchok?! Tagia lepo achshav ata sho-mea oti, ACHSHAV!!* [Yes, Amirkeh, where are you? . . . Then why aren't you coming inside? Tell me what? Is this Dannah who's putting this nonsense into your head? What are you talking about—"New York"? You're getting drafted next week, are you joking? Get in here, now! You hear me? NOW!!]

[*A beat.*]

Unbelievable. It's that girlfriend Dannah, putting this non-sense in his head, with all these trance parties and hashish. She wants to take him to New York—when? Tomorrow! To do what? To *clean carpets*!

[UZI *sighs; he gets quieter.*]

Even if he did not want to go to 669, okay . . . even if he wanted to be a *jobnik* in Tel Aviv, pushing the papers and the pencils, I would be okay. But to run away?! After what his brother sacrificed for him, so he could go to these trance par-ties. So he could go to New York to clean carpets and then have a place to come *back* to when the Americans kick him out for having no visa! The Americans don't want you there,

Amirkeh, why are you going where you are not wanted—to make a few extra dollars?!

No, he is coming, he is coming. He called me from the corner. He wanted to "prepare me" so I will tell him it's okay. Well, it's *not* okay.

[UZI *sadly watches Amir approach the café, a far cry from Gadi, his combat hero.*]

I can see him crossing the street . . . looks like he is walking backwards.

I'm tired. Too tired to be angry. One son is—

[*Explosion. A massive blast rips through the space. Screams, chaos, shattered glass. A middle-age woman wails in pain; an injured young man calls out desperately for his brother.*]

[*The café goes dark as a death light beams down on* UZI, *whose heavy head falls onto the table with a thud. His portly body oozes off the chair and onto the ground. He slowly removes his clothes, resigned to his fate, and crosses toward the upstage right table.*]

[*Light change. As a rendition of "Blue Suede Shoes" and animated sounds of a large family at a Passover seder grow louder and louder,* ALMA YALIN *comes to life.*]

[ALMA, *forty-two, is a tall, slim, chain-smoking Israeli expat with striking features, jet-black hair pulled into a tight ponytail, jet-*

black clothes, and a hint of nouveau-riche perfume. With much flair she tosses a purple pashmina over her shoulders, puts on large designer sunglasses, and inserts a cigarette into her well-manicured fingers. ALMA tries very hard to hide her Israeli accent when speaking English, but her rolling Israeli r's are invincible. Her highly affected speech also involves inadvertent emphasis on all the wrong syllables.]

[*Café lights up.*]

[ALMA *waves to Christiane, cigarette in hand.*]

ALMA YALIN: Excuse me, could we have the bill please? *Helleaux*— Could we have the bill, please?
    [*Smiling*] Oh, I thought you were the manager! [*Walking back to her table*] What was I thinking? An Israeli would never look so professional!

[ALMA *sits down, lights a fresh cigarette. She talks to Christiane as if she were an old confidante.*]

Horrible place, isn't it? It's like third world. Moti wouldn't come back here if I paid him, and he has to take care of the business. Moti's Limousines, largest in tristate area. You should call us when you are in New York!

[ALMA's *cell phone rings. She looks at the caller ID.*]

Oh, it's my sister Shosh. I've only been here two days, I can't wait to get away. [*Into the phone*] *Helleaux*. Hi, Shosh. I am sitting at a coffee shop. I didn't know I was supposed to leave you a note. I told you, Shosh, it's easier for me to speak in English. Well then you talk in Hebrew and I'll answer in English. No, I cannot stay till Friday, I'm leaving on Thursday. Shosh, I'm leaving on Thursday. If you drive me crazy I'm going back tomorrow! Bye.

[ALMA *looks back up to Christiane.*]

You are from London, right? I *love* London. Ach, it's so loud and smoky here, I can't stand it. Trust me, the only reason I am here is because my mother is sick. And I told Shosh, "I will fly both of you first class to New York, we have better hospitals there. But she said, "No, Ima is too sick to fly," and she kept nudging, so finally I said, "Okay! But I'm not flying El Al, with those smelly *dosim* with their black hats and *peot* praying for God to save them!"

[*A man approaches.* ALMA *looks up, slightly annoyed.*]

I'm sorry, do I know you? [*Her face lights up*] Yoni Kahana—oh my God! [*To Christiane*] A childhood friend, how crazy! [*Back to Yoni*] How are you? Manhattan is fantastic! What, are you still living in Dugit, in Gaza? No, I don't watch the news, it's too depressing. [*To Christiane*] The government kicked them out, did you know this?

[*Back to Yoni*] So what are you now, in temporary housing? Wooooowwww. You should come to New York, drive the limousines for Moti.

You are like Shosh, suffering here for no reason. You know she still has the toilet where you have to pull the rope to flush? She should get what we have, superflush technology; you don't have to do anything *and* it plays music. So every time Moti is in there I hear "Blue Suede Shoes."

I am here because my mother is very si— oh, everyone knows everything here.

Oh, you are? No, Shosh didn't tell me. No, I won't be here for that, I'm flying back that night. I know it's Rosh Hashanah, Yoni, but that's the best time to fly; nobody's on the plane.

[ALMA's *cell rings, just in time.*]

I really need to get this. Okay, it was good to see you. [*Looking at the caller ID with enthusiasm*] Who is this?

Oh my God, Naama. I remember the number from when we were children—she hasn't moved since, can you believe it? How did *she* know I was here, I'm like the Queen of England I am telling you—

[*Answering*] Helleaux! Hi, Naama, so good to hear you! No, it's easier for me to speak in English, it comes more naturally [*Pronouncing it "na-too-ra-lee"*] . . . Oh, you *are*? No,

Shosh didn't tell me. No, I won't be here for that. I am flying back that night, I got a good deal on Lufthansa . . . [*Annoyed*] I'm sure she'll be fine without me. [*Smiling forcedly*] Okay, it was good talking to you, bye-bye.

[*Beat. She looks back at Christiane, still irked.*]

It's like everyone is in your *veins* here. "Alma come over, Alma come play dominoes, what are you doing for Rosh Hashanah?" I played dominoes in the army—I've moved on! It's like someone put a message on the radio [*rah-di-yo*], "Alma Yalin is coming back to Israel after fifteen years, let's make her feel horrible!" Let's make her feel like she has forgotten her family, when it is *they* that choose to live in this crazy place. Can I help it if I like living in America? That I can't stand it here! Just because you are born somewhere, does not mean you have to stay there! We go to Lincoln Center every week. We get a table at Nobu like *that!* [*She snaps her fingers.*] Do you know how hard it is to get table at Nobu like *that?!*

[ALMA's *cell rings.*]

Ach, I only come here and I get agitated!!

[ALMA *answers, at her wit's end.*]

Ken, Shosh! Amarti lach, I can't change the *kartis,* it's too expensive *lehachlif et ha* ticket!!! Bye! [*Hanging up*] Oof! Ach! Woww!

[*She takes a long drag of her cigarette.*]

My parents were never big on holiday dinners anyway. My mother hated to cook, and when she did it was horrible. It's a miracle Shosh knows how to cook. And how she has time taking care of our mother all the time, but that was her choice! I told her, I will pay for the best old-age home in Israel, but she said, "No, I'll do it." You know why? She is thirty-eight and has no husband—it gives her focus [*foh-koose*]!

[*A beat.*]

The only good thing about our holiday dinners was my grandfather, Saba Yechezkel. He would take us out on the grass, the mosquitoes would eat our legs, the purple lamp zapping the stupid ones. "I was thirty kilo when I came to this country!" he said. He didn't tell us why he was only thirty kilo, but we didn't want to hear about Auschwitz anyway, we were only ten years old. "I was thirty kilo but I had the strength of an ox. The country looked like shit, but we were so happy to be in the sun, we worked until we collapsed, singing the whole time. The Arabs made fun of us but still they made us coffee." I don't know if I believe that part, but it sounds nice . . . And then he would sing.

[*Christiane asks if she could sing for her.* ALMA *laughs, embarrassed. She starts to quietly sing "Erev Shel Shoshanim," slowly losing herself in the memory, her singing gaining force with every note. She stops herself.*]

Ach, I sound horrible. All these years of smoking . . .

[*She holds back tears. Her tone is softer now.*]

He said, "Every tree, every flower, was like a drug to us." And then he would take the leaves of the *za'atar* plant and stick it up our noses and we would laugh so hard. And then my mother would yell, "Okay, dinner is ready!" but nobody would move because we knew how bad the food was going to be! [*Laughing*] Even my grandfather, who had no sense of taste at his age, said the meals in the *camps* were better! Ima didn't like that joke . . .

After he died, she gave me all his records. No, I left them for Shosh, I only took one with me. Sometimes I listen to it, but very quietly—we live in a very sophisticated neighborhood in Long Island, people like their quiet. It's very civilized. Shosh would go *crazy* living there—she likes people, noise, activity. When we were children, she would listen to his records at full volume, the whole *neighborhood* could hear! Naama, the woman who called me a few minutes ago, she was singing to these records from four blocks away! She had the voice of an angel . . . It changed after her husband died in *miluim* in Jenin.

That's when I told Moti we were leaving this crazy place. I wasn't going to worry about him every time he went to do reserves in Lebanon, or to protect some stupid settler. People like Yoni that think it's okay to live in the *middle* of the Palestinian land. It's their land, let them live, poor souls! Life is hard enough for them as it is! There are a million places to live, you have to live right there?! I will let my husband die for their idea? Life is more important than an idea! It's not 1948 anymore, the swamps are drained! I will let my children die for this idea?!

[*She nods.*]

Yes, two. [*Smiling*] A boy and girl. Cassidy and Dylan. You want to see photos?

[ALMA's *cell rings again.*]

Oh, it's Moti, thank God! [*Into the phone*] Helleaux. Hi, Moti. I'm sitting at a coffee shop with a good friend from London. Yes, I had to leave the house, Shosh was driving me crazy. She is having a big Rosh Hashanah dinner, she invited Yoni Kahana, Naama, remember them? They are coming out of the woodworks! You know thirty people came to pick me up from the airport—I felt like the Queen of England! [*Hopeful*] Maybe *you* can come pick me up from the airport for once, ah? Instead of sending Hector with the limo?

No, of course I'm kidding . . . Of course I'm kidding.

Ehh . . . Friday. No, I thought the flight was on Thursday but it's actually Friday, I made a mistake. I know, I know— I'll have to be here for that, but don't worry, I'll survive. You know, Moti, can I call you right back? Okay.

[*To Christiane*] Excuse me for one minute!

[ALMA *dials excitedly.*]

Shosheleh? Ani nisheret! [I'm staying!] How expensive can it be to change a ticket? [*Choking up*] But you have to promise to make the *of bagril* [grilled chicken] that Saba used to love. And I want to hear his records full volume, blasting through the *ceiling*—

[*Explosion. A massive blast rips through the space. Screams, chaos, shattered glass. A child screams for her mother; a man groans; bystanders rush over.*]

[*Death light on* ALMA, *whose head is thrown back with force. Her body stays frozen for a beat, her cigarette dangling from her dead fingers. She then slides swiftly and smoothly off the chair to the ground, the pashmina fluttering off her body. She approaches the strollers behind her.*]

[*Light change. As we hear the sounds of gusts of wind in an olive grove, trees being chopped down, New York City traffic, and a rabbi*

singing the Hebrew funeral prayer "El Maleh Rachamim," SHULI
FEINSTEIN *begins to form.*]

[SHULI *is a petite, Orthodox, right-wing extremist powerhouse of a
woman in her early thirties. With manic gusto she puts on her mod-
esty-maximizing outfit: a long blue skirt, a light-blue beret that
covers her entire head, and a dated, high-collared, button-down
shirt. She speaks with a hyperalert zeal; her Brooklyn accent has
stayed intact despite her many years living in a West Bank settle-
ment. At times she appears grounded, at times fanatic. Her hands
are always wildly expressive, her body a rock.*]

[*Café lights up.*]

[SHULI *pushes two strollers into the café, talking sweetly to her seven
children while scanning the café patrons.*]

SHULI FEINSTEIN: Look at all these lost souls, pretending the
land Hashem gave us is not on the verge of destruction! Do
you know why—Alma, Batia, Gadi? Why they're lost but do
not realize it? Why they think they can sit here sipping
espressos like they were on Fifth Avenue? Because they have
no leader, neither in Hashem above nor in human form. One
of their leaders was going to sell us out, and look what happened to him. And look what happened to the leader after
that. It's only a matter of time before that idiot Olmert is
taken care of.

[*To the patrons*] Who do you people think you are? Betraying our covenant with Hashem, who promised us this land and peace and security if only we follow his commandments. Do you not realize how you are desecrating Hashem's name by surrendering the land he promised us, bowing to international pressure— [*Spotting Christiane and the crew*] Get that camera away from here! I'm no idiot. You're just out to make more pro-Palestinian propaganda. Out to make us seem like some fanatics, because we happen to know that this land is ours!

Oh, I'm sorry, I'm sorry, you don't believe in God, right? Therefore the Bible is not legitimate justification that this land belongs to us. Okay . . . well, how about a little history lesson, *maideleh,* because I have no problem overturning the ridiculous historical claims the Palestinians have so miraculously fabricated to serve their goal, which happens to be the annihilation of Israel! Oh, and please, keep the camera rolling. And check all these facts, I'm sure you'll find they're *highly* accurate.

[SHULI *looks directly into camera, burning the lens with her stare.*]

Number one: There was never a nation or a civilization referred to as Palestine. No distinct language, or culture, or customs. The very notion that a Palestinian nation has an ancient connection to the land of Israel is one of the biggest lies these people have created!

Number two: There was never a Palestinian state governed by "Arab Palestinians," not even a national movement of sorts until 1964, led by Yasser Arafat, who was an Egyptian!

Number three: We are the only people, the ONLY people that have had a continuous presence on this soil for the past three *thousand* years.

Ask any archaeologist, ask him to show you Palestinian artifacts, he won't have any to show you. Ask him to show you Jewish artifacts, he will beam with pride from his extensive collection!

There was a mighty Jewish empire that spanned this entire region thousands of years before Islam was even *born,* but somehow, the Arabs claim they were the only ones here until Jews pounded on their doorstep right after the Holocaust, how is that not preposterous?

586 B.C.E., we had our Temple on the Temple Mount. The Jews were overrun by Nebuchadnezzar—those that were not expelled, and allowed to remain, rebuilt the nation of Israel and a *second* Temple on the Temple Mount. In 70 C.E., the Romans came, destroyed the Second Temple, and slaughtered most of the Jewish population. And although conditions were horrible and unbearable, still thousands of Jews remained here and rebelled for *centuries* so they could rebuild the nation of Israel in the Holy Land, the promised land.

Oh, and by the way, in 636 C.E., when Arabs came and rooted out many Jews, they did not sit and form a "Palestinian nation." They were just a hodgepodge of Arabs that happened to settle in a geopolitical region called Palestine. They usurped land from the Jews, not the other way around!

Look, I'll be honest with you. I'm not a big fan of secular Zionism, it only takes one look at these half-naked Israelis to know why *Moshiach* has not arrived.

But I will tell you this, when the Zionists came here in the nineteenth century, wanting to live *alongside* the Arabs that were here, the land was foul, neglected. Nothing but swamps and malaria. The Zionists bought this land—legally, mind you—they didn't usurp or steal, and they broke their backs working it, turning the swamps into forests, deserts into fruit-bearing fields, a neglected land into a land of prosperity.

All of a sudden the Arabs decided it was a nice place to live! Ninety percent of the Arabs that emigrated here arrived in the last hundred years! But they were just unemployed outcasts from Jordan, Syria, Iraq, Egypt, that came here and simply seized plots of land. They couldn't find a job in their own country, they looked around, and ended up here! How's that for a strong national and spiritual connection?

What maddens me, *maideleh,* is the greed involved. Arabs control *twenty-two* nations, 99.5 percent of the entire Middle Eastern region. Israel makes up one half of 1 percent of that region. But still it's too much for them! Because we are a Jewish stain. And so they will kill us until every last inch of soil is theirs.

[SHULI *turns to the patrons, emotional.*]

Israel is not some random chunk of land that can be parceled out and negotiated. It is the biblical *and* historical homeland of all Jews, and none of you have the right to relinquish the God-given birthright given to all Jews and to all future generations of Jews!!!

[*She turns to Christiane.*]

Oh, I'm talking to them because it is our Jewish brothers and sisters that will lead to our demise. We are being sold out by traitors that care more about the enemy's human rights than the fate of their own people!

How many more Jewish women and children will die because of their compassion for monsters? Said Rabbi Shimon Ben-Lachish, "He who is merciful unto the cruel is destined to be cruel unto the merciful."

[*Suddenly, to Alma*] Get your cigarette smoke out of my son's face. [*To Christiane*] Of course all these kids are mine—what kind of stupid question is that? Seven: Alma, Batia, Gadi, Dalia, Hershel, Zichron, and Itchak, who's gonna be two months old tomorrow. Say hello, kids!

[*The kids smile and wave.* SHULI *leans in and leads them in a chant.*]

What are we protesting?
Withdrawal!
What else?
Peace talks!
Why?

Because we have to get rid of these bloodsucking murderers before they destroy us!

Dalia, don't punch your brother like that—

[*Explosion. A massive blast rips through the space. Screams, chaos, shattered glass. A teenage boy searches frantically for his girlfriend; ambulances roar to the scene.*]

[*Death light on* SHULI *as she collapses onto the strollers, trying to shield her babies from the blast, to no avail. She vigorously tears the burning clothes off her body, finally draping her long skirt over the toppled strollers, like a baby blanket that has lost its purpose.*]

[*Light change.* SHULI *turns away and heads toward the downstage center table. As we hear the sounds of a chain saw on wood, an espresso machine, German industrial music, and some Billie Holiday,* HENDRIK NIGGEMAN *begins to form.*]

[HENDRIK *is a balding, doughy, German man in his late thirties, with an oddly shaped body. He meticulously puts on a hip leather jacket, horn-rimmed glasses, and a cabbie hat.* HENDRIK *speaks in a quiet drone, each word melding into the other; the result is somehow more jarring than mellifluous. He sits with his back to the audience.*]

[*Café lights up.*]

[*Christiane approaches* HENDRIK.]

HENDRIK NIGGEMAN [*turning slightly around*]: No, I do not want to be interviewed, thank you.

[HENDRIK *goes back to sipping his espresso. Christiane does not relent.*]

No, I am not Israeli. I will be of no help.

[*She asks again.*]

Look, I'm very sorry, but my boyfriend Daniel is going to be here any minute . . . He is Israeli, yes. I don't know what his political leanings are, we never talk about it.

[HENDRIK *realizes Christiane's not going anywhere.*]

Scheisse.

[*Turning around fully to face her*] We met in Germany many years ago. He was there on a high school student tour, to "meet the Nazis," as he likes to call it. He is making a joke of course. My family was not happy about their arrival. At the time my father was fighting a big battle against Jewish reparations, you know to give Jewish families German money. Well, why should our generation give them money? We did nothing wrong. Germany has to tend to its own problems: crime, education, things like that.

So I, Hendrik Niggeman, fat with bad skin, that had never been a leader of *anything*, I organized a protest of about forty people to "meet" the Israeli bus as it arrived. My father was so proud of me, he did not call me fat or ugly once that whole week!

Daniel was the sixth one off the bus. He had dark skin, dark blue eyes, and dark curls like I had never seen before, a beautiful creature. I immediately had an erection, my first ever! Daniel smiled at me, which only made my erection bigger, and harder for me to keep my GO BACK TO ISRAEL! protest sign up.

Before I knew it, I had joined their tour group!

I was so enamored with Daniel I even went through the nightmare of going to Bergen-Belsen just to be with him. Oh, please, we hated going to these camps. Once was enough. We were so tired of seeing photos and class trips and lectures on what we have done, it's in the past. There is enough going on in the world to not shove the Holocaust down our throats! Trust me, Daniel agreed with me—for the rest of the tour we just stayed in my bedroom.

[*He giggles.*]

That killed my father on several levels. But in reality he was too busy fighting immigration to worry about his fat, ugly son fucking an Israeli boy . . .

We stayed in touch for many years after that, and after Daniel finished his army service, I asked him if he wanted to come to Berlin to live with me in my studio. And he did! I taught him how to make furniture with me; mostly plywood, sometimes fiberglass. He was a natural. His pieces were so powerful—they were functional and emotional at the same time, like the pieces were fighting the air for oxygen. [*Throwing his hands in the air dramatically*] Pah, pah, pah!

We were so happy together . . . Then one morning he woke me up and said, "I am going home." I remember that morning like it was *this* morning. Daniel always had very strong morning breath, of sleep and cigarettes. I miss that smell, horrible as it was, with him it was sexy.

"I thought this was home," I told him. I didn't understand. Daniel never had any strong connection to Israel, no interest in political events . . . We had gone to a club the night before and there was a tiny *Hakenkreutz*—eh . . . swastika—graffiti on the wall, but it was nothing. Daniel got upset but I calmed him down later with cognac and a blow job!

Maybe I didn't calm him down, I don't know. Maybe he had Holocaust guilt and wanted a nice Israeli boy. Within a week he was back here.

Life became unbearable. Our conversations were so painful . . . Israelis are very honest, you see. I would ask him, "Miss me?" and he would say, "Not really." So after a while I just told him how much I missed him without waiting for an answer. Then one day he said, "It is better if we do not speak anymore."

I cried every day like a baby. It was winter in Berlin, and all the furniture I was making looked warped, twisted, hollow materials ... all my pieces were like bodies in pain, writhing, empty inside.

Ironically these pieces were doing very well. My biggest hit was the Daniel chair. I purposely designed it so that it made you feel unstable, that it could break at any moment if you sat on it the wrong way, teetering on the brink of collapse.

Two people were killed by these chairs. They did not read the warning. They were old and half blind, but you should not buy modern furniture if you cannot read the warning!

Regardless, I knew I was becoming dangerous. I was designing a new table with an edge so sharp it would slit your wrists if you leaned on it.

So I got on Flight 007 to Ben-Gurion and I called him. I was so nervous to hear his voice I could barely breathe. He was surprised to hear from me, which made me very angry. Here I was in a sobbing lump in Berlin for six months, and he was here, living with some man, and they were happy. They even came to pick me up from the airport together. Very tall, handsome, stupid man. Still in the army. Thinks he is big shot because he gives orders to young boys. "Oh, you have such big responsibilities, you have people's lives in your hands, I only design furniture. But you do not love Daniel like I do! Yes, you look the same and you can speak Hebrew to each other and your grandparents weren't Nazis, but Daniel and I transcended those gaps—our love was not based on familiarity or comfort; ours was a primal connection, sex, a mutual love of art!"

Well, of course I told him this, but it didn't work. So finally after weeks of begging and crying, I said, "Okay, Daniel, I am going back to Berlin!"

Then I rented an apartment a few blocks away from here.

Praying that the stupid boyfriend would get killed by a car. And I could go to Daniel and console him . . . I could be there for him as he mourned someone else, and every time I would visit, I would bring a pair of underwear and then shirt and pants and before he knew it I'd be moved in, and we would start our new life together!

But bad luck. No car accident. Instead I'd watch them every morning as they'd walk their dogs in the park and then come to this café and have espresso. His stupid boyfriend would always order a big salad with feta cheese, and every time he would take a bite, a piece of feta would fall on his lap. Like a handicapped child! Daniel thought it was so cute. I had to make sure I didn't vomit from the corner from where I was watching them.

The hardest part was that he didn't recognize my work. The chair he was sitting on *every* morning in this café was my design and he didn't realize. You see, [*caressing the chair*] it has my signature curve—it hugs the body, makes it feel warm, comforted, loved. I call it the Israel chair. It is my first design inspired by him, and I reverted back to it when I moved here. Hoping for a self-fulfilling prophecy, perhaps. Now that I look back, I think I should have put the Daniel chair here instead.

Four years, yah. I have been here four years . . .

You think I am pathetic, it's okay, so does my family. But last week, I ran into the boyfriend.

[*He smiles mischievously.*]

He was in uniform, big Uzi on his shoulder. He looked at me and said, [*in dumb guy voice*] "Aren't you Daniel's friend from Germany?"

"Yes." I said. "I live right around the corner."

"Oh. I used to live here too."

"Where do you and Daniel live now?"

"No, Daniel still lives there. We broke up a month ago."

"Oh, I'm sorry to hear that," I said, immediately feeling an erection.

"Yes, I have to say I broke his heart."

"Oh, that's too bad. Good to see you, bye-bye!"

And then I ran straight to Daniel's apartment. He wasn't home so I left him a note. "Meet me at Montefiore Café, one P.M."

[*Excited, desperate*] Oh, no, he will be here! And I will take him into my arms, make him feel warm, comforted, loved, and he will *never* leave.

[*Beat.*]

Do I have coffee breath? Daniel hates that—such a double standard, you know how it is!

[HENDRIK *cups his hands around his mouth and tries to do a breath check.*]

Ugh, this never works. I only end up smelling my hands. I think I am okay, yah?

[HENDRIK *exhales.*]

[*Explosion. A massive blast rips through the space. Screams, chaos, shattered glass. Firemen hose the site; paramedics tend to the injured.*]

[*Death light on* HENDRIK *as he twitches, grabbing onto his Israel chair for mutual support, as if it were his dying mother. Once on the ground, he removes his clothes with the same pedantic care as he had put them on.*]

[*Light change. As the sound of sexual grunts, snowstorms, and Russian music float through the space,* SVETLANA, *a Russian prostitute in her early thirties, begins to form, seductively donning a midriff-baring sequined top, micromini, and "fuck-me" heels.*]

[SVETLANA *is tall and leggy, and has short, bleached-blonde hair, ample breasts, and a deep voice that's part raspy, part nasal, tinged with a heavy Russian accent.*]

[*Café lights up.*]

[SVETLANA *meanders among the tables, eyeing possible clients. Bingo.*]

SVETLANA [*to the potential john*]: You want to meet me in Hilton hotel? Two hundred shekels an hour. Come on, you look lonely. Of course you wear condom, what you think because you were big shot in army you have no diseases? What about my diseases? You know who was inside me already? Boris . . . Shmulik . . . Igor . . . Chezi . . . Igor—these are different Igors by the way—Shimi, Yevgeni, Vitush, Daniel, Ofer, Alek, Anatoli, Andrusha, Antosha, Arkadij, Chezi, Arnon, Bogdashka, Bolodenka, Borya, Eyal, Danya, David, Avi, Shimon, Danny, Dima, Erez, Felix, Ilia, Yasha, Kolenka, Leonide, Lukasha, Max, Pashenka, Rani, Sacha, Ariel, Dudu, Vina, Yakov . . . Yuri . . . Zevik . . . Petr . . . And that was only Monday. Now you wear condom? Smart man.

[SVETLANA *leads her client to the exit. Christiane walks toward them.*]

Can't you see I'm busy?

I don't have political opinion, I don't give shit. If things get too crazy, I go back to Moskva, finish my Ph.D. in *fisica*.

No, I am telling you I don't give shit. You think immigrants in America give shit about country? They are only there to make money so they can buy BMW and show off in old neighborhood.

[SVETLANA *realizes the potential john has walked off.*]

You see, now you scare away client. Ach, it's been so quiet lately. When there was war in Lebanon they come running to me for release, now it's dead quiet.

I come here because the men are nice and the coffee is fantastic. It makes you shit in the morning without having to have cigarette. But cigarette never hurt. It's funny, I don't like cigarette after sex, you like cigarette after sex? [*Assessing Christiane*] You like sex? Look at you, I don't think so.

Of course I like sex. You have to like sex if you like this job. Most girls I know like this job. We get to do what we want, many times a day, and we get paid for it. Of course, some men are smelly and disgusting, but I have special system, it's called "shower."

No, Israeli men are horrible lovers. But they fuck great. They have fire, passion, anger. The army teaches them to be like macho animals. They tell me under all the macho bullshit they are very tender, but I don't buy it. I don't need tender, it's okay—I have enough chupi-muchi from my husband, Maksim.

Are you kidding? He loves that my vagina is a highway. Who do you think bought him his Mercedes taxi? I told him, "If you don't start making money you will have to find another prostitute wife to have sex with, because I cannot deal with such impotence; you are useless, useless!"

It was his idea to come here. Yes, it's easier than Europe, for work. The Israeli government is so happy Jews want to come live in this crazy country, does not matter what you want to do. You want to be Jewish crack dealer, they will tell you, "Please, come sell crack here, fantastic! The Arabs are outnumbering us. Boohoohoo, boohoohoohoo!"

They give us health care, tax break, *stipendia* . . . They almost give me client list!

No, don't be silly, we are Christian.

[*She pulls out the cross necklace that's been resting in her cleavage.*]

At first Maksim said, "*Shhh*, Svetlana, you have to keep that secret." I said, "Please! It's good for business!" Israeli men feel less guilty when their whore is not Jewish. And it's exotic for them, I think it's exotic!

No, we pay a guy in St. Peterburg fifty dollar to make paper that says we are Jewish. You know it's so funny—we pay a guy to make paper that says we *are* Jewish. When in history this is happening, ah? [*Laughing*] Never in history!

You know, it's so easy to fuck the Israeli system, which is big irony, because Israelis are *masters* of fucking the system. They are such combination of naive and suspicious.

The men, they always haggle with me over fucking price, but they never haggle before we fuck; they haggle while they are coming inside me, as if I will be so distracted. "Oh, Shmulik, you are so gooooood! Here, please take fifty-shekel discount, please! Please!"

I have never met people like this. They have hope in something they know is impossible. They have hope in life of peace, but they are smart enough to know it's never going to happen. How can you hope for something you know is not going to happen?

I think it's because they are like wounded animals; they don't know left from right, right from wrong. They are like, "The world treated us like shit, now we treat them like shit! Look who's boss now, hahahahaha!"

I don't know . . . Maybe that's what happens when you are hated your whole life. A kid is hated one year in school, he is traumatized for life. These guys have been hated since the beginning of time. Before there was anybody on the planet . . . the *dinosaurs* hated the Jews. Look at the Americans—they get bombed once and *opp!* they become the most suspicious *bezumets* on earth! But for me, I don't care, for me work is work, a place is a pla—

[*Explosion. A massive blast rips through the space. Screams, chaos, shattered glass. Police bark orders, instructing all bystanders to clear the area.*]

[*Death light on* SVETLANA *as she flies to the ground. Her legs now useless, she crawls on her hands and elbows toward the upstage right table, removing her scant clothing unsexually in the process, her high heels dragging along the café floor.*]

[*Light change. As an eerie tone, like a choir gone awry, resonates through the space,* TREV BRODMAN *begins to form.*]

[TREV *is a very chubby, very cheery, very devout American Christian evangelist in his fifties. He wears a festive, checkered button-down, short-sleeved shirt. He speaks slowly, with a heavy southern accent, enjoying every syllable that drips out of his mouth, and grins constantly regardless of what he's saying.*]

[*Café lights up.*]

[TREV *is leaning on a table, his butt and belly both somehow sticking out at the same time. He's on the phone with his Israeli business partner.*]

TREV BRODMAN: Well, it's disrespectful, Shmulik, is what it is. I mean, how bad can traffic be, you have a Vespa! Well, if I'm talking to a pretty brunette reporter, wait till I'm done, okay?

She's been scoping me out for the past twenty minutes, I can tell she's dying to talk. Okay, buddy, get here soon.

[TREV *spots Christiane and struts her way like an overweight peacock.*]

[*Calling out*] Ma'am. Ma'am! I see you walking around lugging that big heavy microphone, I can't help thinking, "Gosh darnit, she must be tired, walking around lugging that big heavy microphone!"

[TREV *flashes a toothy smile.*]

Trev Brodman, pleasure to meet you! Oh, no, no, please join me, he's gonna be late.

You have beautiful eyes. Are you Israeli? You do have a semblance of Mediterranean in you, right? I can tell you don't burn. Speaking of burning, so good of you to capture this country's final days on camera. I mean with Israel's neighbors closing in on her like this, it's only a matter of time before we all [*making little wing motions toward the sky*] boop, boop, boop, boop!

"For the Lord himself shall descend from heaven with a cry of command, with an archangel's call and with the sound of the trumpet of God. Those that are dead in Christ shall rise first, then we who are alive, who are left, shall be caught up together with them in the clouds to meet the Lord up in the air and so we shall always be with the Lord!"

We have funneled a great deal of money and political support towards Israel's security efforts because we have to ensure that Israel stays in the hands of its rightful owners. The Israelites must rule this land in order for Christ to return, and we must protect them from harm until the battle of Armageddon!

Well, at that point they either accept Jesus as their savior or get incinerated.

That's not to say we won't do everything we can to bring our Jewish brothers and sisters into the light. Part of the center is a recruitment hub of sorts.

[TREV *proudly unrolls some architectural plans sitting on the table.*]

Well, this here is the Mount Zion Rapture Center. Masterpiece of architecture. Twenty-one square miles. The main entrance is a huge glass atrium with windows onto the heavens. We call that the "destination room." And once you pass through it, you enter a seven-mile-long corridor, along which is an interactive journey through the life of Jesus, unlike anything you've ever experienced.

Imagine yourself walking down this corridor, barefoot, with only essential clothing on your body . . . hot coals under your feet . . . sharp nails along the walls on which you will rub your palms against as you walk past . . . the deafening sounds of Armageddon *blasting* through your ears—sounds of demolition, destruction, annihilation, incineration, torture! You will be sweating and panting and crying, but you'll have to keep going, cuz there's no turning back. But don't worry, we'll be there to help you along when you encounter difficulty.

[TREV *breaks into a comforting smile.*]

[*Christiane inquires about another spot on the blueprints.*]

[*Proudly*] Oh, this here, this is a memorial for all the Jews that will perish in the Rapture. It's just a courtesy really, cuz after all, it is a choice.

[*Another huge smile.*]

[*Pointing*] And this here, this here is a gift shop, which is gonna be right where you're standing, isn't that neat? Oh no, not at all, this will all be long gone by then!

    Oh noooo, the Israeli government could not be more welcoming and friendly! They've been putting us up at these fine hotels, *amazing* breakfasts, and I can't help thinking, "Gosh! What an amazing people! They *will* see the light; they *will* change their ways!" And we will have so much more fun in heaven, cuz they're a colorful, feisty bunch, it'll be great to have that energy up there. [*Whispering*] My wife, Cheryl, bores me to tears. I can't imagine dealing with *her* for all eternity. Keeps telling me how stupid I'm being, how the

Israelis don't believe in the Rapture, how they're just using us for our money and political support.

Cheryl gets a kick out of putting me down, but that's okay. The Lord has blessed me with very thick skin. And lots of it! [*Laughing*] My older brother Steve used to call me every name in the book. He only kept me around cuz I was bigger than him, I'd scare the bullies away. Nobody touched Stevie Brodman when Trev was around, that's for sure! I was his security wall, kept the terrorists out. And the girls out, too. They ended up going for the larger specimen, if you know what I mean.

[TREV *winks.*]

Cheryl doesn't know that, of course. She thinks I was a virgin when we met, just like she was. I told her, I said, "Cheryl, honey, I'm not stupid. I'm aware of the 'situation.' Shmulik told me straight up, he said to me, 'Trev, we Jews need all the help we can get, if it's from a bunch of "wacky" Christian fundamentalists that think that Israel's destruction is imminent, well, as long as they're willing to help us until then, we'll play along!'"

So I asked Shmulik, I asked him straight up, I said, "Is it really smart to rely on people that think your only option is to convert or die? It's not smart—it's actually sorta dangerous and let me tell you why . . . Our Rapture theology predictions

are *malleable.* The book of Revelation is full of graphic imagery, but it doesn't really explain what that imagery means
and is no way a clear blueprint for what the future holds—
not like these blueprints here you see. Now, Shmulik, what
might happen is, these 'wacky Christian fundamentalists' that
have been so crucial to your government—not to mention
your tourist industry—they may start getting antsy when the
Rapture doesn't happen as soon as they thought, and they
may start *reinterpreting* Revelations to justify the holdup.
Now what if that new interpretation is that it is the very *ex-
istence* of Israel that's causing the delay? That the new
Jerusalem cannot descend until the old Jerusalem is destroyed first to make room for it?

"It won't be long before they start concluding that a *different* kind of Israel has to exist for the Rapture to occur, an
Israel occupied entirely by its Arab neighbors, let's say. Arabs
that have been suffering sooo much for sooo long . . .

"You know what happens then, *Shmulik?* That powerful
ally you've come to love and utilize, it will *shift,* will pull the
rug out from under you. All those nifty new Christian friends
you made at those luncheons and conventions, they'll start
luncheoning and conventioning with your enemies, finding
new ways to expedite the process of your destruction. And
your people will wake up one morning and find themselves
all alone, with no big brother Trev to protect them. Cuz the
truth is, big brother Trev would slaughter every last Jew on

the planet if it meant the Lord would take his worshipping body up to heaven! [*Breaking into a laugh.*] But don't worry, buddy, we're all good for now—"

[*Explosion. A massive blast rips through the space. Screams, chaos, shattered glass. Remaining survivors are loaded into ambulances.*]

[*Death light on* TREV, *who looks up at God beaming down on him and smiles at his savior. He removes his shirt and baseball cap with glee and walks toward the upstage right table.*]

[*Light change. Warm, fluid, womblike sounds and a heartbeat bring to life* REBECCA, *a sweet-faced, doe-eyed nineteen-year-old, who meekly puts on her army uniform.*]

[REBECCA *has a nervous, insecure energy about her. Her voice is lodged somewhere in the back of her throat, occasionally journeying through her nasal passages. She speaks both English and Hebrew with a heavy American accent, at a volume higher than she's aware of. She unconsciously fiddles with her army sweater cuff throughout.*]

[*Café lights up.*]

[REBECCA *walks hunched toward the downstage center table, nervously carrying a tray of four mugs of coffee. She looks up at Christiane.*]

REBECCA: *Selicha, at yoshevet po?* Oh, I'm sorry are you sitting here?

I am, actually, a sergeant, yeah. Oh, sure! Do you mind if I just put these down first? I can't afford to get another uniform dirty, the name-calling on base is bad enough as is.

I'm from the Upper West Side. But my parents weren't rich, if that's what you're thinking. My mom was an only child—actually, both my parents were Holocaust survivors who moved to America before I was born. Yeah, they were really old when they had me. It's a miracle I didn't come out all brain damaged or anything!

I'm just kidding. I'm not a negative person. I get bitter about stuff sometimes but I never take it out on other people. I hate when people do that, you know? They're having a bad day and then they take it out on you, and they think it's okay. They're like, "I know I'm being an asshole, but I'm having a bad day." Well, I have a lot of bad days and I never take it out on *anybody.* Then they make you feel stupid for being hurt by their behavior, they're like, "Don't be so oversensitive, don't be such an *Amerikakit!*"

Amerikakit, yeah . . . That's what my commander, Yossi, calls me. Get it? American—kaka, kaka—American. He thinks it's the funniest thing in the world. I want to be like, "You know what, dude—that's not cool! I know you think all Americans are stupid, but you wouldn't be here without America. This country is *nothing* without America! And you know what? I didn't have to serve in this army—I'm an

American citizen, I volunteered instead of going straight to college. I had nobody here, no friends, no family. I mean were *your* parents fifty when they had you?! That are both dead?! Are you all alone in the world?!"

[*Catching herself*] Sorry. I promised myself I wouldn't get too emotional today, I don't want to come off as too desperate, I don't want to scare them away. Chana and Naama—these two women. They claim to be my mother's sisters, but she never mentioned them.

Yeah, they live in Petah Tikva. It means "gateway of hope." It's kind of a shithole, but I guess it's the intention that counts.

Well, we talked briefly on the phone, and they told me how my mother was transferred to a death camp, and how they were sure she was gassed, and she was sure they were gassed, and then after the war they looked for her in Israel and then they gave up. They couldn't fathom that she didn't *come* to Israel after the war, which is a whole other issue, to be perfectly honest. I don't know why she didn't come here either. All my life she kept pushing the importance of a Jewish homeland in Israel and then she moved to New York! I mean, if it's so important the Jews have a country, then why weren't we in that county?!

[*A beat.*]

They died within a month of each other, my parents. As if the minute one was gone there was no reason for the other to keep me company. I know that sounds ridiculous and I don't feel sorry for— Well, actually I do feel sorry for myself. But I'm allowed. Orphans are allowed. Real orphans, none of these dime-store orphans, with a brother or sister or uncle in Minnesota!

I guess that's why I came here, to find a family in the Jewish people. I guess I thought the land of the Jewish people would welcome me with open arms, kind of like a second-generation Auschwitz survivor. I wasn't expecting *Amerikakit*.

Anyway, these two women found me, I don't know ho— Well, actually I do know how. There was an article in *Yedioth Ahronoth* about volunteer soldiers and they interviewed me. [*Proudly*] I guess I made a good story: "American orphan volunteers for intelligence unit." And there was a big photo of me, and Naama said she recognized me immediately. I look exactly like my mother. It's kinda freaky, really, we're just clones of our parents. We look the same, chances are we have the same height, weight, intelligence, glaucoma, life expectancy . . .

Anyway, they wanted me to come over for a family dinner, with their kids and their grandkids and I totally didn't want to go. I mean what was I gonna do there? Sit there uncomfortably watching strangers' kids running around? Making noise, *parents* everywhere . . . flying rice and spilled sour cream . . .

But they kept *calling*. I guess they felt guilty they never really bothered to track my mom down after the war. I mean one Google search they would have found our address on Riverside Drive—my mom had her own piano-teaching business, we weren't *that* hard to find.

Maybe they didn't have a computer, I don't know.

Anyway, I told them I couldn't come to dinner because I was stationed up north and I rarely got off base. But they kept *calling*, and they kept saying, "What would your mother have wanted you to do?!" which made me angry because my mother's dead—how the fuck am I supposed to know what she would have wanted me to do? She never even mentioned these women! I mean here she was thinking she was all alone in the world, and they were here living these festive lives in the gateway of hope and now they're pulling this shit on me?! And I said that to them! Which made me feel empowered, kind of like I was pissed off on my mother's behalf. I don't get to be pissed off very often—one wrong word to Yossi on base and I'm fucked. He once kept me on base for *eight* weeks straight. Any other soldier would have contested, but he knows I don't have a boyfriend, or family waiting for me, or anything . . .

God. I sound like a whiny bitch, don't I? Sorry. It's just that I haven't had a heart-to-heart with a woman in . . . ever. No, Israeli women are very cliquish. They're very confident, sexual, arrogant. They all have boyfriends that are in 669 or pilots or *Duvdevan*. Nobody wants the *Amerikakit*. Especially if she's not blonde or easy or has big [*mouthing*] boobs. I mean, I look Israeli but I'm not, so I don't have the perks of either nationality.

You know what's really ridiculous? They keep making fun of Americans, but they can't stop talking about how the minute they're released they're going to New York! How they can't wait to get away from their suffocating families [*putting her hands on her neck*]: "*Machnik po! Machnik po!*" Like a womb that chokes them.

[REBECCA *tries to hold back her tears.*]

I tell them I don't know what it means to be suffocated . . . I think it sounds kind of nice.

[*Her floodgates open.*]

Maybe my mother would have wanted me to be suffocated for a while—maybe that's what these women meant when they said, "What would your mother would have wanted you to do?" . . . [*Sobbing now*] She wouldn't want me to be alone . . . I hope.

So I called them. After six months I called them back . . . and they were so happy to hear from me. All I could think was, "Why did I wait so long? Here are these women that want to suffocate me."

[REBECCA *smiles through her tears, a four-year-old trapped in an eighteen-year-old body.*]

Well, they're picking me up in four hours. [*Embarrassed*] I'm a little early . . . That's a lot of coffee to drink. [*She takes a needy sip.*]

[*Explosion. A massive blast rips through the space. Screams, chaos, shattered glass. Members of Chevra Kadisha* arrive on the scene, begin collecting body parts.*]

[*Death light on* REBECCA, *who falls onto her back. She struggles to remove the sweater from her jittery body, then curls into a tiny fetal ball.*]

[*Light change as trance music starts seeping in through the din.* AVIVIT, *a lean, energetic, colorful, Goa raver chick in a colorful bandeau top bounces up from the floor like a firecracker.*]

[AVIVIT, *twenty, is a joyous being, full of life energy. Her voice is high-pitched and bubbly, floating on a river of giggles; every new word is as exciting to her as the last.*]

[*Café lights up.*]

[AVIVIT *dances between the tables, handing out psychedelic flyers.*]

AVIVIT: Party for peace, *exta chinam im ha flyer!* Party for peace—*exta chinam im ha flyer!* [free ecstasy with this flyer!]

---

* Chevra Kadisha is an organization of religious Jews who have taken upon themselves the responsibility of collecting severed limbs and pieces of skin after suicide attacks so as to try and fulfill the Halachah (Jewish law) of burying a corpse in its entirety.

[AVIVIT *suddenly spots the camera crew and hides her face behind her flyers.*]

Oh, please move the camera! My brother will kill me if he knows I said ecstasy on television! Interpol is chasing after him all over Amsterdam. They think he is the biggest ecstasy dealer in Europe. [*Proudly*] He is! He is lucky to have a sister like me to help keep the business running! If I could call Interpol I would tell them, "Interpol, why are you chasing after my brother when he is trying to do good, trying to bring peace?" He is not selling crack, or weapons, or cocaine that makes you think you are king of the world, he is selling ecstasy, it's a drug of love—it's the solution, I am telling you—what is your name? Christiane. You are looking very locked-up inside, straight like a box. This flyer will get you one free ecstasy pill and a backup pill if you need it, if you have high metabolism or you are fat.

[AVIVIT's *phone beeps.*]

Ah, sorry, SMS from Walid! [*Reading excitedly*] He has already covered ten villages and is going to Khan Younes. *Sachten!*
    Walid is our business partner. His whole family is our business partner, all over the West Bank and Aza. His brother and my brother are best friends in Amsterdam, and together they decided to build a network to bring ecstasy into Israel because we are such a good market here!!

They ship the *exta* to Egypt, the Egyptians give it to Walid in Aza—oh no, that's easy—the Egyptians will let anything through if they are getting paid for it.

Oh, how he gets it from Gaza to me? It's a secret, you want to know? The tunnels, that the terrorists build, from Aza into Israel. Walid finds out where the tunnels are from his friends that are digging them, and he sends a messenger and I send a messenger and we make the exchange!

Well, why should only the bad guys use them—why can't the good guys use them?! No, it is the army's job to find the tunnels and capture and kill the terrorists, it's not helping! There are hundreds of tunnels, there are hundreds of terrorists! We are working for a real solution—to change the terrorists' minds. A party for peace!

Last week we got a thousand hits of *exta* for the party. My brother called me and said, "Avivit, you have to do the pickup, I don't trust anybody but you for this one!" So I went to the tunnel to meet the messenger, and when he came out, I knew it was Walid!! [*Gushing*] His voice matched his body, you know? He was a virgin, can you believe it?? It was very rough, our sex, right there in the field! Pushing, pulling my hair, grabbing my shoulder. He was swallowing me, my heart, my soul, and I was swallowing him, his anger, his love. So much love! Walid says we are like Romeo and Yulia, Gaza style!

It was his idea, this party for peace. A party to bring Palestinians and Israelis together, because we cannot rely on our leaders for a solution.

No, they are good people with passion and ideas, but they have too many memories, too many scars, that make them angry and childish, with big ego. Only through common enjoyment, not common suffering, can we come to a solution, a party for peace!

It's been very hard. Nobody wants to come. Walid has been talking to his friends in the mosque, the university, the angry ones that want to kill us, and he says, "Wait! There is a better way! What would you prefer—a smile on your face and new furniture or a crying mother and your bones angry underground?"

Finally I said I will pay them! For every ticket an Israeli buys for two hundred shekels, I am giving a Palestinian two hundred shekels to come to the party. And now we have eight hundred people coming!

[AVIVIT *dances excitedly. Off of Christiane's look, she slows down, perplexed.*]

You are so cynical. What kind of life can you have when you are so cynical? An ugly one, I think.

Imagine yourself at this party, in a field in the forest, with five hundred people you love and five hundred people you hate. You are on two sides of this field. The only sound you hear is the sound of the music, and you are moving to it because it is natural. The ecstasy has put a smile on your face, you are smiling at your friends, they are smiling at their friends . . . And you are all moving to this one beat, because there is only one beat . . . By now, the ecstasy is all in your blood and you cannot fight it. It is a chemical that is telling your brain, "I am happy, I feel good. The people around me feel good. I hated them before, but I can't hate them now, they are smiling at me. Look, one of them is dancing close to me. [*Gasping*] His skin has touched my skin. His breath is warm, his touch is pleasant. I love this person. I do not want to hurt this person. I want this person to be happy all the time because *I* want to be happy all the time."

No, the *exta* is just a push, because we are so low right now, we have to bring everybody up to a baseline. And it will fade, but the memory of the experience will not! [*Dancing full-on now*] The pleasure with the other persons will remain, and it will be impossible to go back to the hate that was befo—

[*Explosion. A massive blast rips through the space. Screams, chaos, shattered glass. A cumulative cacophony of all the explosions and their aftermaths.*]

[*Death light on* AVIVIT *as she continues to dance for a few beats, slowly losing her coordination as death tingles through her body.*]

[*Light change. As the sound of Arabic oud music and Chopin nocturnes blend beautifully together,* AVIVIT *stumbles toward the downstage right table where* NIJMA AZIZ's *well-pressed black blazer awaits.*]

[NIJMA *is a regal Palestinian professor in her late fifties, with a gentle, quiet demeanor. She calmly and elegantly puts on the blazer and takes a graceful seat in the chair, facing the audience straight on. She crosses her legs under the chair and clasps her hands.*]

[NIJMA *is eloquent, her speech is remarkably even and measured, her voice quietly authoritative and compassionate. Her accent hints of a European education.*]

[*Café lights up.*]

[NIJMA *smiles politely.*]

NIJMA AZIZ: I only ask that you not put me on camera, my colleagues at Birzeit would not be thrilled that I am sitting here.

I am a professor of statistics there, yes. I live in Ramallah but I come here once a week to have coffee. It is not easy, mind you. I wait four, sometimes five hours at the checkpoint, get patted down, harassed, depending on what kind of day the soldiers are having. [*Smiling gently*] They are just kids, really. Some of them have come to know me. They call me Professor; they let me through relatively quickly.

It is tiring, our life. The few hours that I can sit here before rushing back for curfew are like a dream. Here I can sit and pretend my life does not exist. I close my eyes and hear the clanking of the espresso machine, smell the freshly baked pastries—I could be anywhere, Paris, Prague. The conversations around me are about children, money, technology, post-doc programs at Columbia, start-up companies in Herzliya.

Did you know that Israel has more biotech companies than anywhere in the world outside Silicon Valley? Youssef hates when I tell him that. [*Smiling*] My son, yes. I tell him, "That cell phone you are talking on, Youssef, was actually developed in Motorola Israel. The ICQ—the instant messenger where you are sending your friends messages of anger and hate—was created by two Israeli boys. Look at the opportunities these people have created for themselves, opportunities we can create for ourselves also!"

He says I am spitting on my own people, with these stupid statistics. That we are not lucky enough to be the paid puppets of America.

I understand where he is coming from. How can we attain such accomplishments when we are occupied? Bombed, harassed, tortured, unable to feed our own children, let alone "start a start-up"?

"Yes, Youssef, occupation has bled us dry, but what are *we* doing to remedy? Look who we put in power. Yes, they have built us a few clinics, but they have no value for this life, why would they try to better it? They are focused on the next life, where they hope to not be such impotent victims."

I cannot blame him. I cannot blame our youth. Hate overpowers every other thought process in their brain. From the first day Youssef was in school, posters of martyrs surrounded him. He is taught to not take responsibility for his despair, to not blame our own leaders, but to focus his anger on the "real enemy," the people sitting here laughing while we drown in sewage-filled streets.

It is like a bad marriage. My marriage. My husband and I always blamed the other for our despair. Always demanded the other change their behavior first as a "precondition" to changing our own. It is human nature to avoid responsibility and put the onus on the other, but the only way to live well is to control what *you* can control, to be proactive toward a place of prosperity, not of revenge!

[*Chuckling wryly*] No . . . The only person Youssef hates more than me and the Israelis is my husband. He left us many years ago, to go teach at the Sorbonne. They offered me a position as well, but I wanted to stay here, in my home-land, to be a native, a local. No matter how hard my husband tries, he will never be a true Frenchman, not in the French eyes—to them he is just another dirty Arab living in France. That is where we and the Jews are the same in Europe!

It is a bit crazy, my decision to stay here, considering the life Youssef could have had, the opportunities. My husband says I wanted a struggle, to feel noble by fighting a fight. But I have lost faith in those that are fighting it. And they see me as a snob, a traitor who was educated abroad and has no real connection to her people. [*Ashamed*] The truth is, I would rather sit here surrounded by those that my people consider the enemy. It is a sad state to be in, let me assure you. Youssef assures me *all the time.* He says . . . [*this is difficult for her*] I am like a mother who prefers to play with the neighbor's healthy happy children and leave her own crippled ones screaming in pain at home.

No, it is too late for that. Youssef will never leave now and I cannot leave him here alone to be sucked in by his friends' anger and thirst for blood. They are like hawks.

[*Desperate now*] I want to give my son a cohesive Palestinian identity, but that is proving difficult when I also keep telling him that we and the Israelis are the same—we are all human!

How can he transcend nationalism when that is the only thing he can call his own?! He has nothing. He has seen his friends give their life pointlessly, every house on our block demolished, a wall built around us to cage us in like *animals*. That is the Israeli stupidity.

I refuse to let my son reach a point where his life is so bleak he is willing to give it up. That is why I asked him to join me here for coffee. I said, "Youssef, please just once, join me here for coffee!" My friends at Tel Aviv University, they are so eager to display their extremist left-wing pro-Palestinian minds, they have even arranged for his smooth passage!

I believe that showing him a life of normalcy and prosperity will not lead to bitterness or resentment, but to hope and inspiration, for even though these people look like monsters to him now, their journey was not an easy one.

[NIJMA *spots Youssef walking into the café; her face lights up.*]

Ahh, there he is! Such a handsome boy! [*Proudly*] I bought him that suit, very expensive, Armani.

[*Youssef stops, notices Jessica.* NIJMA *watches, amused.*]

Oh, he is looking at that girl. I knew he would think Israeli girls were pretty up close.
Oh, look, she is smiling at him.
Oh, he is going to talk to her! [*Happily, to herself*] Youssef . . .

[NIJMA *realizes what's about to happen, she leaps out of her chair, horrified.*]

Youssef!!

[*Silence. Death light on* NIJMA *who stands there, frozen.*]

[*Blackout.*]

ACKNOWLEDGMENTS

Many thanks to Professor Mano Singham for his insights into the Rapture. Trev's remarks on the book of Revelation as a blueprint for the future and the risk of Israelis' reliance on evangelists are taken from his Web Journal, with his permission, and paraphrase quotes from Gene Lyons and Chris Hedges about protecting the Israelites from harm until the battle of Armageddon.

Shuli's claims and rhetoric are culled and paraphrased in part from the speeches of Rabbi Meir Kahane, the Arab American journalist Joseph Farah, Chabad Lubavitch–related Web sites, www.newswithviews.com/israel, and various newspaper articles.

UZI KARABELNIK: "I said, 'You Americans are so funny, you have one war in Vietnam, you are making five hundred movies about it.'"

ALMA YALIN: "Moti wouldn't come back here if I paid him . . ."

TREV BRODMAN: "You do have a semblance of Mediterranean in you, right? I can tell you don't burn."

REBECCA: "Nobody wants the *Amerikakit*."